Inside My Body

Why Do I Burp?

Isabel Thomas

Chicago, Illinois

www.heinemannraintree.com
Visit our website to find out more information about Heinemann-Raintree books.

To order:

☎ Phone 888-454-2279

🖳 Visit www.heinemannraintree.com to browse our catalog and order online.

© 2011 Raintree
an imprint of Capstone Global Library, LLC
Chicago, Illinois

Edited by Kate de Villiers and Laura Knowles
Designed by Steve Mead
Illustrations by KJA-artists.com
Picture research by Mica Brancic

Originated by Capstone Global Library Ltd
Printed in the United States of America by Worzalla Publishing

15 14 13 12 11 10
10 9 8 7 6 5 4 3 2 1

Library of Congress Cataloging-in-Publication Data
Thomas, Isabel, 1980–
  Why do I burp? : digestion and diet / Isabel Thomas.
    p. cm. — (Inside my body)
  Includes bibliographical references and index.
  ISBN 978-1-4109-4014-8 (hc) — ISBN 978-1-4109-4025-4 (pb) 1. Digestion—Juvenile literature. 2. Digestive organs—Juvenile literature. 3. Belching—Juvenile literature. I. Title. II. Title: Digestion and diet.
  QP145.T43 2011
  612.3—dc22   2010024679

Acknowledgments
The author and publisher are grateful to the following for permission to reproduce copyright material:
© Capstone Publishers p. **7** (Karon Dubke); Corbis p. **25** (© Paul Souders); Getty Images p. **5** (Photonica/White Packert); Getty Images News pp. **13** (isifa/Libor Fojtik), **26** (Jasper Juinen); NASA p. **27**; Photolibrary p. **10** (Juniors Bildarchiv); Science Photo Library pp. **14** (Eye of Science), **17** (Susumu Nishinaga), **18** (Eye of Science), **21** (Scimat), **22** (Scimat), **9** (3445128471); Shutterstock pp. **15** (Eric Gevaert), **23** (Sascha Burkard).

Photographic design details reproduced with permission of Shutterstock pp. **4**, **19**, **22** (© Isaac Marzioli), **4**, **19**, **22** (© Yurok).

Cover photograph of girl with hand over mouth reproduced with permission of Corbis/Retna Ltd./ © Rena Durham.

We would like to thank David Wright for his invaluable help in the preparation of this book.

Contents

Words that appear in the text in bold, **like this**, are explained in the glossary on page 30.

Why Do I Burp?

You're finishing off a meal when you feel something bubbling up from deep inside. Your hand clamps over your mouth just in time. BURRRRP!

When you eat and drink, you swallow small bubbles of air. This air gets trapped in your **digestive system** (the rollercoaster of tubes that food travels through after you eat). The air is squeezed as you eat and drink more. Finally the trapped air escapes, making a loud noise on its way out.

Practical advice

Blame it on the food

Burping three to four times after a meal is normal. You might burp more if you eat too quickly or drink through a straw, since you will swallow extra air.

Air is not the only **gas** that gets trapped in your digestive system. Other gases are formed as food travels through your body. Trapped gases that cannot escape through your mouth travel through your whole digestive system and exit from your bottom!

Getting these trapped gases out of the way is handy, because your digestive system has an important job to do. It breaks food down so that your body can use all the good stuff locked inside. This process is called digestion.

🔍 **Fizzy drinks can cause big burps because they contain extra gas. The little bubbles of a gas called carbon dioxide gather in your stomach before bursting back out.**

Why Is Digestion Important?

Food needs to be broken down before your body can use it for energy and growth. The useful substances in food are called **nutrients**. Each type of nutrient does a different job in your body.

Your **digestive system** has to break down chunks of food into **particles** of carbohydrate, fat, and protein that are tiny enough to travel in and out of **cells** and zoom around in your blood.

Your digestive system is made of several different zones. Throughout the book, this diagram will help you to discover what your food faces in each zone.

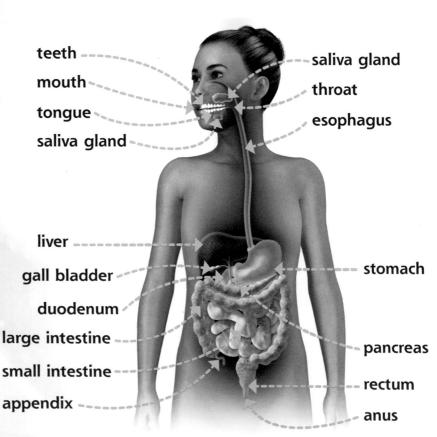

teeth

mouth

tongue

saliva gland

saliva gland

throat

esophagus

liver

gall bladder

duodenum

large intestine

small intestine

appendix

stomach

pancreas

rectum

anus

This book will take you on a tour around the digestive system. Climb on board the digestive rollercoaster to find out how your body breaks down food to get at the nutrients inside. Watch out for the things that make you burp!

🔍 **The nutrients found in foods are the building materials for cells. You couldn't live without them.**

Foods such as bread and pasta contain sugars and starches (also called carbohydrates). They provide instant energy. Your body uses energy all the time, even as you sleep.

All foods contain **vitamins** and **minerals**. These do special jobs that keep your body healthy.

Fruits and vegetables contain a lot of water. Your food provides a fifth of the water you need each day.

Meat, fish, eggs, and beans contain proteins. Proteins carry out complicated tasks such as carrying messages around your body, killing germs, and building muscles. Special proteins called **enzymes** even help to digest food.

Milk, cheese, and butter contain fats. Fats keep your body warm and cushion your organs from bumps and bangs. They also release energy slowly, so your body keeps working even if you have not eaten for a while.

How Does Digestion Start?

Seeing, smelling, and even thinking about food kicks your **digestive system** into action. Saliva glands squirt saliva (spit) into your mouth, ready for the first bite.

Teeth are specially shaped to help break food down. After your front teeth bite off a chewable chunk, your tongue pushes the food around your mouth. The flat-topped back teeth crush and grind it into smaller pieces.

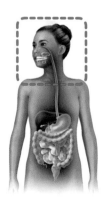

teeth

mouth

tongue

saliva glands

throat

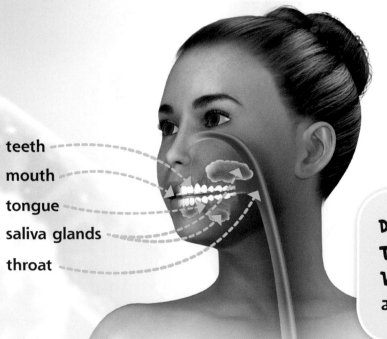

DIGESTION ZONE: mouth
TIME: 20 seconds
WATCH OUT FOR: biting and grinding teeth, saliva

What does the tongue do?

Your tongue is covered with tiny bumps that send information about food to your brain. Some are spiky, gripping and moving food as you chew. Other bumps detect whether food is hot or cold, rough or smooth.

The bumps are also home to up to 8,000 taste buds that tell you if food is sweet, sour, salty, bitter, or **umami**. Along with sight and smell, taste tells your body if food is safe to eat.

Eating the same thing every day would be unhealthy—and boring! Our sense of taste allows us to enjoy a range of foods.

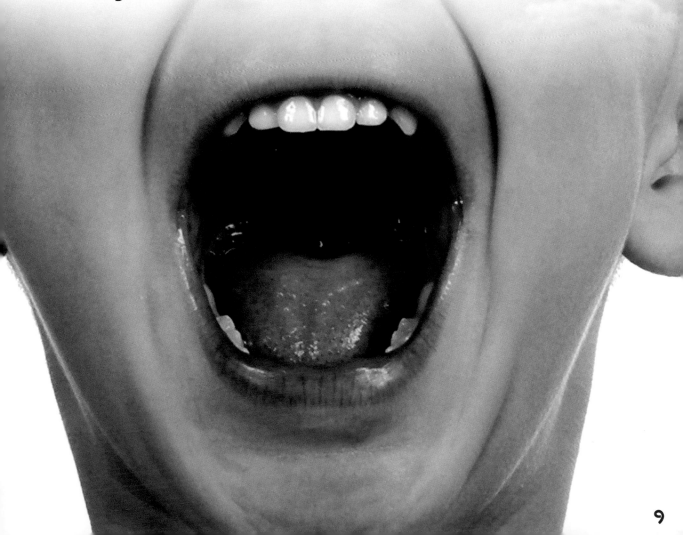

What Does My Saliva Do?

So far your food hasn't had much fun. It has been pushed by your tongue, crushed by your teeth, and soaked in slimy saliva.

🔍 **Digestive enzymes are very powerful. Tarantulas don't need to chew. Instead, they inject saliva into their prey. Enzymes in the saliva dissolve the victim's insides, turning it into a soup that the tarantula sucks up.**

Saliva is also packed with proteins called **enzymes**. These help your body to break food down more quickly. Enzymes grab onto chemicals in the food and split them into **particles** too tiny to see.

A sweet taste

Different enzymes attack food as it travels through your **digestive system**. Each one breaks down a certain type of food. The enzyme in saliva begins to digest starch, turning it into tiny particles of sugar. As the sugar washes over your tongue, food starts tasting sweeter.

Chewing mixes your food with saliva, making it softer. The **mucus** in saliva gives food a slimy coating so that it can be easily swallowed. Your tongue pushes a bolus (ball) of soft food to the back of your throat. A long tube called the **esophagus** leads the way to your stomach.

SCIENCE BEHIND THE MYTH

MYTH: The only cause of bad breath is not brushing your teeth.

SCIENCE: Brushing your teeth is important, but did you know that a dry mouth can also cause bad breath? Saliva freshens your mouth by killing bacteria that build up on your teeth. So, make sure you drink plenty of water.

What Makes a Burp So Noisy?

Your **esophagus** moves food from your mouth to your stomach. Food does not just fall down the pipe. Muscles in the esophagus walls squeeze together and push the ball of food toward your stomach. It is kind of like pushing toothpaste out of a tube!

This swallowing action even works if you stand on your head. Food is moved through your whole **digestive system** in the same way.

DIGESTION ZONE:
esophagus and stomach
LENGTH (esophagus):
25 centimeters
(10 inches)
TIME: 2-3 seconds;
4-6 hours
WATCH OUT FOR:
squeezing walls, sudden
burps, acid, churning

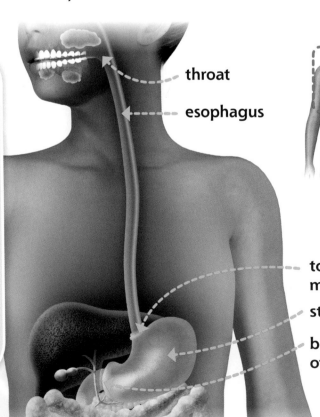
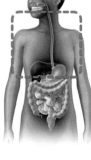

throat

esophagus

top ring of muscle

stomach

bottom ring of muscle

Extreme body fact

Record-breaking burp

Paul Hunn produced the world's loudest burp in 2008. His 107-decibel belch would damage your hearing if you stood too close. Paul did it by contracting his abdominal muscles to force gas out quickly.

The muscle to blame

At the bottom of the esophagus, a ring of muscle opens to let food into your stomach. It closes again to seal the food inside. You can blame this muscle for noisy burps. When trapped **gas** escapes from your stomach, it bursts through the ring of muscle. The muscle vibrates (moves from side to side) like the neck of a balloon when air escapes. The vibrations make a noise.

Air might be able to escape from your stomach, but your food is not so lucky. Read on to find out what it faces next.

What Happens Inside My Stomach?

Your stomach has two jobs. Super-stretchy walls let it store big meals, so your body can digest the food slowly. Your stomach also kick-starts digestion by mixing food with **gastric juices**.

The walls of your stomach are covered in gastric pits, which squirt food with a sticky combination of **mucus**, acid, and enzymes.

Gastric juice

Little pits in your stomach's lining pump out around 1.5 liters (2.5 pints) of gastric juice every day. This is not the kind of juice that you would want to drink. It contains **enzymes** and a strong acid. The enzymes start to digest proteins. The acid kills nasty germs that may have hitched a ride on your food. It also helps the protein-chomping enzymes to work.

Strong muscles in the stomach walls toss everything around like a cement mixer. This turns your meal into a sloppy paste. If you have ever thrown up, you will know exactly what this paste looks like! There is a ring of muscle at the bottom of your stomach. It opens to let the paste squirt through, a little at a time.

Extreme body fact

Burping is not green
Cows are the world's biggest burpers. They burp methane **gas**, which is formed as grass is digested in their four stomachs. Methane is one of the gases that cause global warming. There are so many cattle farms that cow burps release more global warming gas than the world's planes, trains, and cars!

What Happens in My Small Intestine?

The small intestine is a long, narrow tube coiled up beneath your stomach. It is here that your body finishes digesting and then **absorbs** (takes in) the **nutrients** in food.

The duodenum is the first part of the small intestine. Here the food is drenched in digestive juices from the **pancreas**, and bombarded by bile from the gall bladder. These juices continue breaking down fats, proteins, carbohydrates, **vitamins**, and **minerals** into tiny **particles**.

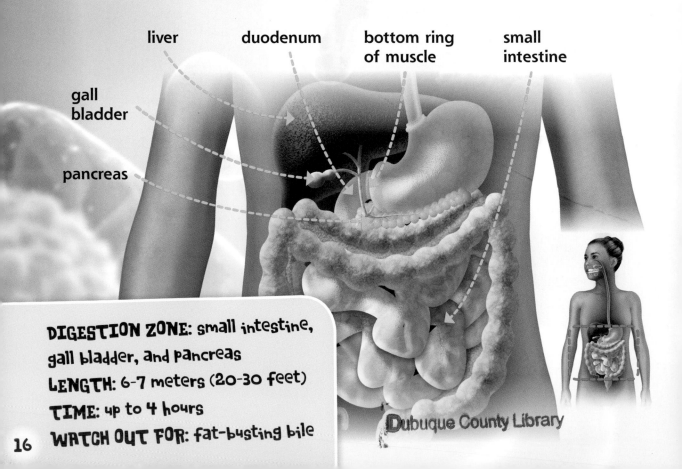

liver

duodenum

bottom ring of muscle

small intestine

gall bladder

pancreas

DIGESTION ZONE: small intestine, gall bladder, and pancreas
LENGTH: 6-7 meters (20-30 feet)
TIME: up to 4 hours
WATCH OUT FOR: fat-busting bile

Super enzymes

Enzymes are the intestine's secret weapons. As food passes into the small intestine, extra enzymes squirt out from glands in the intestine walls, along with water and **mucus**.

Bile is a green digestive juice made by the liver. It is stored in the gall bladder until the body needs it. Bile breaks fats down into tiny droplets, like dish detergent dissolving grease in a pan. Enzymes can lock onto these droplets to break them down further. The thin, watery food mixture is now full of food particles small enough to pass through the intestine wall.

The intestine walls are crisscrossed with blood vessels that are ready to absorb all the nutrients from the digested food.

Extreme body fact

Your **digestive system** breaks food down into particles that are 10 million times smaller than a lump of swallowed food. This is the same as breaking Mount Everest down into grains of sand.

How Does Food Get into My Blood?

The "small" intestine is actually the longest part of your **digestive system**. It provides plenty of space for your body to **absorb** all the **nutrients** in food.

The intestine lining is not smooth. It is covered with millions of tiny "tentacles" called villi. These tentacles increase the **surface area**, so there is even more space.

🔍 **This is a magnified image of villi. These tiny parts give the small intestine a surface area as big as a tennis court.**

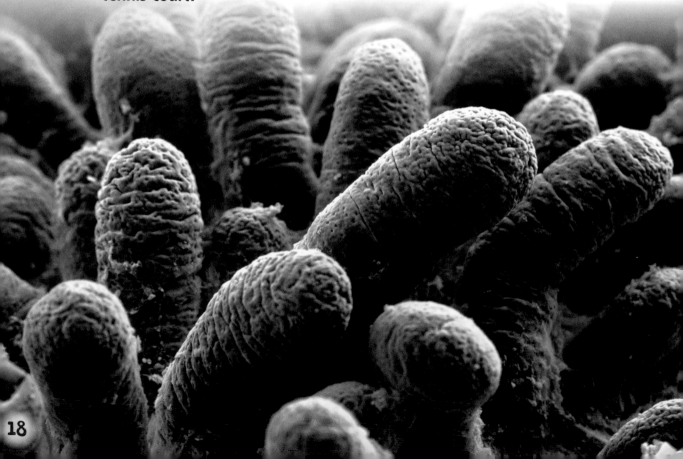

Most types of food **particle**, as well as water and **minerals**, are absorbed through the small intestine wall and into the blood vessels that surround it.

Once nutrients are in the bloodstream, their first stop is the liver. This huge organ sorts out the nutrients so that your body is not flooded with food after a meal. Some nutrients are stored. Others are put back in the blood and sent around the body. Harmful substances are removed. The **pancreas** helps out by making a substance that controls the amount of sugar in your blood.

Practical advice

How do I know when I'm full?

As you eat, your digestive system sends signals to your brain, making you feel full. This is your body's way of telling you to stop eating. It can take 15 to 20 minutes after food is first eaten for all these signals to get to the brain. If you eat too quickly, force yourself to finish large portions, or choose too many foods high in fat and sugar, you may take in more food than you need.

What Happens to Food My Body Can't Use?

Not everything that you eat can be digested. **Enzymes** cannot break down many substances found in plants. These substances are known as fiber.

The leftover material moves into the large intestine (which is shorter but fatter than the small intestine). Your body is careful not to waste anything useful. Water, salts, and some **vitamins** are **absorbed**.

DIGESTION ZONE: large intestine and rectum
LENGTH: 1.5 meters (5 feet)   **TIME:** 1 to 3 days
DIAMETER: 7 to 10 cm   **WATCH OUT FOR:** billions of bacteria

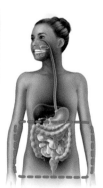

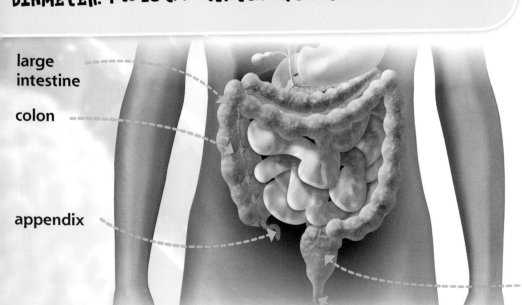

large intestine

colon

appendix

rectum

anus

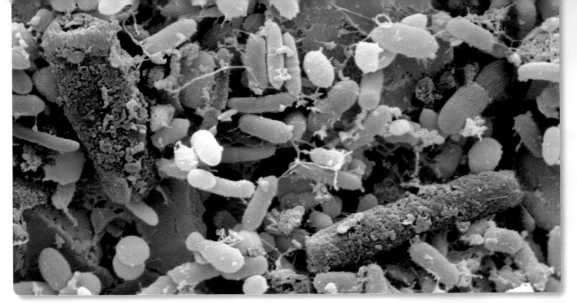

Billions of bacteria live in your digestive system and make up almost a third of your feces. They are known as "friendly" bacteria because they help your body to break down food.

Feces

As water is drawn out, the leftover material gets harder. It is now **feces** (poop). It contains substances your body wants to get rid of, such as used-up red blood **cells**. These are passed into the intestine from the liver and give feces a brown color, no matter what you have been eating.

The feces are gradually pushed into the rectum. They are stored here until they have a chance to exit the body by being pushed through the anus, a ring of muscle at the bottom of the **digestive system**. This might happen the next time you visit the bathroom!

Extreme body fact

Bottom burps
If swallowed air is not burped up, it is passed as a **gas**. Most people pass gas between 6 and 20 times a day.

What Happens If I Eat Something Bad?

Germs such as bacteria love food. When bacteria find themselves on a plate of food at the right temperature and surrounded by plenty of air, they quickly grow in numbers.

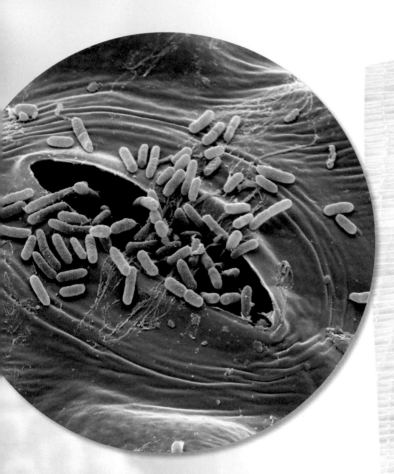

🔍 Bacteria can only be seen with a microscope. These *E. coli* bacteria live on some foods and can cause food poisoning.

Practical advice

Keep your food germ-free

- ✔ Don't sneeze and cough over food.
- ✔ Wash your hands before cooking or eating.
- ✔ Cook and reheat food properly—heat kills bacteria.
- ✔ Keep raw food away from cooked food.
- ✔ Store food in air-tight containers.
- ✔ Keep food cool. Bacteria grow more slowly in a refrigerator or freezer.

Food poisoning

Eating food that has germs on it can make you sick with food poisoning. Your **digestive system** reacts by squeezing food and water out of each end. This vomiting and diarrhea helps your body to get rid of the dangerous food quickly.

Vomiting starts when germs irritate your stomach lining. Sensors send messages to your brain, which tells your **diaphragm** to contract. The ring of muscle at the top of your stomach opens, and a big push forces food up your **esophagus** and out of your mouth. Yuck!

Throwing up is very unpleasant. The **gastric juice** from your stomach makes vomit acidic. It can burn your throat.

🔍 **Houseflies don't mind throwing up. A fly vomits digestive juices onto food before sucking the softened snack back up. This spreads germs very easily—the fly's last meal may have been a steaming pile of feces.**

How Can I Take Care of My Digestive System?

Your **digestive system** works hard to keep the good parts from food and to get rid of the bad parts. Like any machine, it works better if you take care of it. Indigestion, bloating, burping, and hiccups are all signs that your digestive system might need some care.

Eating slowly and chewing food helps your stomach to cope with big meals. Eating too quickly can irritate your stomach and **esophagus**, and it might also cause hiccups.

Extreme body fact

Hiccups for life
When you hiccup, your **diaphragm** contracts quickly, sucking in air. The "hic" is the sound of the flap that separates your air and food tubes snapping shut. American Charles Osborne had the world's longest case of hiccups—from 1922 until 1990!

A healthy diet

You can keep your digestive system working smoothly by eating a healthy diet that includes fiber. You cannot digest fiber, so it gives the muscles of your digestive system something to push on as they move food through your body. Bulky fiber also helps you to feel full for longer.

Your body is nearly two-thirds water. Drinking six to eight glasses of water a day keeps it well supplied. Fiber **absorbs** some of this water, which makes leftover material bulkier.

High-fat foods are difficult for your digestive system to break down. Taking a break from fatty foods helps food to move through your digestive system more quickly.

Cacti are very high in fiber. Broccoli and whole grain bread are better options if you do not have the jaws of an iguana!

How Long Does Digestion Take?

On the digestive rollercoaster your food is attacked by acids, bathed in bile, and ambushed by **enzymes**. Fats, proteins, and carbohydrates are broken down and taken up by your blood. The parts your body does not like are sucked dry and squeezed out. It is enough to make you burp.

🔍 Spain's La Tomatina festival is the world's biggest food fight. About 140 tonnes (154 tons) of tomatoes are broken up without any help from the **digestive system**!

Extreme body fact

Hungry humans
The average person chomps through as much as 45 tonnes (50 tons) of food in a lifetime. That's the same as eating 14 hippos!

Eating in space can be tricky. An astronaut's digestive system has to work hard, too.

Astronauts can't burp
Earth's **gravity** pulls food toward the bottom of your stomach. **Gas** rises to the top, where it can be let out with a burp. There is no gravity in space, so the contents of an astronaut's stomach float around inside. This makes it very difficult to burp. If a burp happens, it may let out some of the stomach contents at the same time.

In just six to eight hours, a meal is transformed into a collection of **nutrients** whizzing around in your bloodstream and helping your body to grow, study, play, and digest the next meal. That's right—it is time to do it all over again.

Your Amazing Digestion

Burping a lot is one sign of indigestion. Watch out for these burp hazards to keep your **digestive system** working smoothly:

Top ten BURP HAZARDS!

- Drinking through a straw
- Swallowing bubbles of air as you eat normally
- Eating too quickly
- **Gases** forming in stomach as food is broken down
- Drinking fizzy drinks
- Stomach too full from overeating
- Exercising too soon after eating
- Stomach acid escaping into the **esophagus**
- Lying down too soon after eating
- Eating too many fatty foods

The digestive system

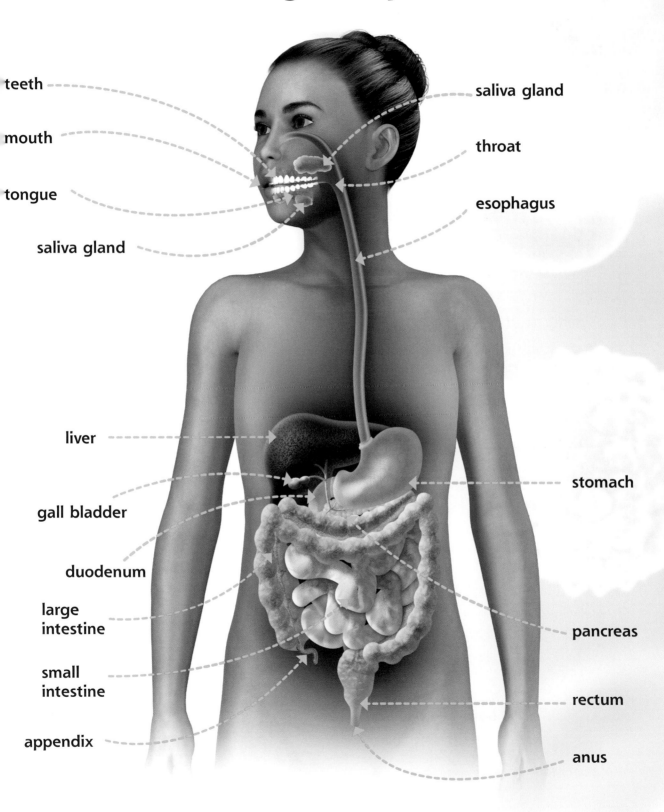

teeth

mouth

tongue

saliva gland

saliva gland

throat

esophagus

liver

gall bladder

duodenum

large intestine

small intestine

appendix

stomach

pancreas

rectum

anus

Glossary

absorb take in

cell smallest part of a living thing

diaphragm large muscle that sits between your lungs and your digestive system, and which controls breathing

digestive system all the organs that help your body to digest and absorb food, and to get rid of undigested food

enzyme special protein that helps your body to break down food into small particles

esophagus tube linking your mouth to your stomach

feces solid waste that leaves your digestive system

gas substance that is not liquid or solid, and that can move around like air. Oxygen and methane are types of gas.

gastric juice fluid released from glands in the stomach lining, containing enzymes and acid to help digest food

gravity force that pulls everything downward toward Earth

mineral natural substance not made by living things. Your body needs minerals to help it grow, develop, and function.

mucus thick, slippery substance that helps your food to pass smoothly through the digestive system

nutrient substance that your body needs to grow, develop, and function

pancreas organ near your stomach that makes digestive juices to help your body break down food as well as a substance to control blood sugar levels

particle extremely small piece of something

surface area outside of something; the part that is in contact with other substances

umami type of savory taste in foods such as meat and fish

vitamin natural substance made by living things. Your body needs vitamins to help it grow, develop, and function.

Find Out More

Books

Barraclough, Sue. *The Digestive System: What Makes Me Burp? (Body Systems)*. Chicago: Heinemann Library, 2008.

Smith, Penny. *First Human Body Encyclopedia*. New York: Dorling Kindersley, 2005.

Websites

http://kidshealth.org/kid/htbw/digestive_system.html

Learn all about the digestive system at this website made just for kids.

http://yucky.discovery.com/flash/body/pg000029.html

Select "Belches and gas" on this website to find all the yuckiest facts about how your body breaks down food. The site contains sound effects and animations.

www.mypyramid.gov

The U.S. Department of Agriculture's website teaches you all about the "food pyramid," which is a guide to healthy eating.

A place to visit

Exploratorium at the Palace of Fine Arts
3601 Lyon Street
San Francisco, California 94123
www.exploratorium.edu

The Exploratorium has exhibits that teach you more about the human body and how it works.

Index